THE GRIDIRON

Thoughts About the Christian Year and Other Things

CLIVE H JACKSON, READER

authorHOUSE®

AuthorHouse™ UK
1663 Liberty Drive
Bloomington, IN 47403 USA
www.authorhouse.co.uk
Phone: 0800.197.4150

Published by AuthorHouse 10/03/2018

ISBN: 978-1-5462-9913-4 (sc)
ISBN: 978-1-5462-9912-7 (e)

Print information available on the last page.

Introduction

When we first had a pew sheet in church, I saw it as a good medium for a little quiet teaching about the faith and what the church is about.

As time passed, people have thanked me for these brief, succinct contributions to the publication and suggested that I should "go into print" so that more people might share them. So, here they are, for your reading. Please read them prayerfully. I hope that in their small way they might deepen your faith, increase your knowledge of it, and stimulate you to ask more questions and to seek answers.

I am particularly grateful to Elizabeth and Rodney, who twisted my arm to prepare this material for publication. Also, I thank them for their help in preparing this material.

The Christian Year: An Overview

The year begins with the season of **Advent,** when we think of the first coming of Jesus into the world and the way in which it was prepared for his coming. Then follows **Christmas,** the well-known and popular festival when we remember the Saviour's birth to a Jewish lady, Mary. This is followed by the **Epiphany,** when the Lord was first shown to the non-Jewish people, the Gentiles. Quite a significant event for those not of the Jewish faith. It is the first recorded time that the Lord was shown to non-Jewish people (Gentiles), reminding us that he came for everyone.

Things move on rapidly to **Lent,** and the Lord's life, which leads up to his Crucifixion.

Appropriately, the solemnity of Lent and Holy Week is followed by the joyful season of **Easter,** when we celebrate the **Resurrection** of Our Lord. Forty days on, and we celebrate the **Ascension** of Our Lord. It is not long after the Ascension that the church celebrates **Pentecost** (or **Whitsun**), when the Holy Spirit of God descended on the church and kick-started it into action—action that continues to this day!

As you may know, the rest of the year, up until Advent, is taken up by the season of **Trinity,** with much teaching and many commemorations.

I hope that you enjoy this tour through the Christian year and that it deepens and makes more relevant your practice of faith in Christ Crucified, Risen, and Ascended.

ADVENT

Many of us enjoy reading novels of one sort or another. People of any age group enjoy reading exciting stories which make the books difficult to put down. In many cases, they tell of people going out of their comfort zones and doing incredibly difficult and challenging things. That's all part of the adventure.

In the season of Advent, we remember an *advent*ure! This refers to when God himself did a very risky thing—he became human, with all that the word *human* means: to be tempted, to lead the life of a "normal boy" subject to the will and discipline of his parents, to get on with his peers and members of the community into which he was born, etc. Also, it means to worship with his fellow humans, encountering "the church" (a Jewish one) of his day, rubbing shoulders with fellow worshippers, and experiencing the life of that church with all its good and bad points.

Today, we celebrate his Advent on the world stage. What exciting challenges faced the Son of God as he grew up in the home of a carpenter in the town of Nazareth. I remember spotting a modern carpenter's shop in Nazareth when I visited.

We are all aware that Jesus came to show us the Way, as well as suffer our punishment, because God so loved the world and us rebellious humans.

So, Advent is a penitential season, which is why we use violet as the liturgical colour in some churches. It is a time for prayerful preparation for the festival of Christmas, and, maybe, a perfect moment for dipping into the scriptures and learning of God's will for humankind. It is with some wisdom that the church directs us to pray for grace so that we may cast away the works of darkness and put on the armour of light.

ADVENT AGAIN!

In the Common Worship daily service book of the Church of England, the service of evening prayer contains the seven Advent antiphons (or anthems) which used to be said or sung before and after the Magnificat at vespers, the evening service of the undivided church. This was discontinued in the Church of England when Archbishop Cranmer prepared the service of evening prayer from vespers and compline. Now in the new service book, they are back!

One of them says, “O Morning Star, splendour of light eternal and sun of righteousness; come and enlighten those who dwell in darkness and the shadow of death.”

So it was that God sent his Son to do just that. But we of the church are now Christ’s body on earth left to enlighten those who dwell in darkness. What are we doing to help the needy and to spread the knowledge of Christ and his teaching in our midst? Through witness, maybe, and through our contact friendship and cooperation with local Christian bodies. Could we engage with other Christians to show that we are all part of the worldwide (or catholic) family of believers?

In the antiphon sung on Christmas Eve, we pray, “O Emanuel, our King and our lawgiver, the hope of the nations and their Saviour: Come and save us, O Lord our God.”

He is there to provide the grace to move things forward. Pray about it.

Not only are there special words to say or sing in the evening, but there are also special words which are sung before the Eucharist or Mass. These are known by many Christian folks as the “Advent Prose”. It is also known as the “Rorate Coeli”, the Latin words of Isaiah 45:8 from the Latin Bible (or Vulgate). They are frequently sung to plainsong and include words from the patriarchs and prophets foretelling the coming of the Saviour:

> "Comfort ye, comfort ye my people, my salvation shall not tarry. Why will you waste away in sadness? Why hath sorrow seized them? Fear not for I will save thee. For I am the Lord thy God, the Holy one of Israel, thy redeemer."

This is a reassuring note on which to prepare for the Christmas festival.

John the Baptist

Appropriately in one of the collects (prayers) used during the Advent season, we ask, "O Lord, at your first coming, you sent your messenger to prepare your way before you." In the readings, we hear from him too. St Augustine, writing in the fourth century, wrote of St John the Baptist: "The voice of one crying in the wilderness, prepare the way of the Lord." Augustine goes on to say that the voice resounds as if it were saying, "I speak out in order to lead him into your hearts. He does not choose to come where I lead him unless you prepare the way for him." To "prepare the way" means to pray well; it means thinking humbly of oneself. We should take our lesson from John the Baptist. He is thought to be the Christ, but he declares he is not what they think. He does not take advantage to further his own glory. He saw where *his* salvation lay. He understood that he was the lamp, and his fear was that it would be blown out by sin and pride. So wrote Augustine all those years ago.

The example of what St John is doing in preparing the way is surely something Christian people can take on board, maybe making it plain by word and deed that we benefit from attempting to love God and to love our neighbours as ourselves. After all, this is why Our Lord came!

Christmas Is Coming!

The build-up to Christmas has become something that is beyond a joke. All the weeks of pressure to spend vast sums of money on presents—for what reason? Hopefully, to celebrate the Saviour's birth in that Bethlehem stable, among the cattle, the sheep, and other animals.

In celebrating Christmas on 25 December, it is all too easy to forget those other souls who are commemorated immediately after Christmas Day. Poor Stephen witnessed to his Lord with great bravery and love, praying for his persecutors as he died: "Lord, do not hold this sin against them."

Then, there was John, who wrote of Jesus, "We are writing these things so that your joy may be complete."

But there were also those children who had done no wrong but were killed because King Herod was afraid that a new king might come and throw him out.

> There was Thomas Becket of Canterbury, who was martyred at vespers in his cathedral.

All these are part of that Communion of Saints to which we profess a belief when we say the Apostles' Creed. They, like us, worshipped and acknowledged the babe of Bethlehem as their God and Saviour.

When it comes, have a happy Christmas!

CHRISTMAS THOUGHTS

The baby Jesus came to a land which had been made part of the Roman Empire (as was our homeland, Britannia). The place of his birth, Bethlehem, is very much visited today by those on holiday or on a holy journey or pilgrimage.

The Church of the Nativity, built on what is believed to be the site where the Saviour was born, dates to the time of Queen Helena, mother of Constantine the Great. Her son, incidentally, was proclaimed emperor of Rome in York, on the site of the present York Minster. Deep in the crypt is where the Prince of Peace was born, marked by a silver star. But Bethlehem is a place divided by an ugly wall to separate the Jewish and Palestinian parts of the sadly divided country of Israel. Modern pilgrims and visitors pass through a heavily defended checkpoint.

The intention of God was that his Son should take on human flesh and show by teaching God's way of love. There are two objects of love: God himself and our neighbours (those with whom we share the planet). The society into which Jesus was born needed to adopt that message and act upon it. What went wrong, then and now? We humans of today need to act upon it as well!

Ephrem of Syria, who lived from about 306 to 373 and was the greatest poet of the early Christian centuries, wrote this:

> At the feast of the nativity let each person wreathe the door of his (her) house so that the Holy Spirit may delight in that door, enter in and take residence there; then by the Spirit we will be made holy.

There are those who believe that being holy means loving God and their neighbours in the same way that they wish to be loved.

CHRISTMAS AGAIN: SCROOGE

"Bah! Humbug!" Those are the two words Scrooge used to describe his attitude towards Christmas in Charles Dickens's book *A Christmas Carol.* That was at the beginning of the story. At the end, having learned a little about people other than himself, we see him with a broad grin on his face as he delivers a goose to his poor clerk, Bob Cratchit, and takes to his heart Bob's crippled son, Tiny Tim. What a change in this grasping old sinner whose god was wealth! Today, people absorb themselves in a variety of objects, clothes, mobile phones, iPads, and motorcars. The list is a long one. Might these, like Scrooge's wealth, be rather like gods to these people?

Sadly, they do not inspire their devotees to look out to those people who share God's world with them. We, at Christmas, celebrate amidst the tinsel and holly the coming of the Son of God into the world to show us a better way forward. It is a way in which there are two parts: loving God and our fellow humans, together with loving the other living things—animals and plants—that share our planet.

At the Midnight Mass or Eucharist, the opening words of the Gospel of St John are frequently read: "In the beginning was the Word and the Word was with God …". *Word* is a translation of the Greek word *logos,* which has a variety of meanings, depending on its use. One such meaning is "the reason why". It can also mean "making sense of". So, the reason why the Son of God came was because God loves us and wants us to make sense of our lives by following his Son. This means having a very different attitude from that of Ebenezer Scrooge at the beginning of *A Christmas Carol.*

The Baptism of Jesus

At first glance, it seems odd that Jesus needed to be baptised. It is difficult to understand why, if the Holy Spirit of God was involved in his origin, there should be need for baptism. But it is clear that the baptism of Jesus marks an important development in the dealings of God with us humans. From the early days, he had concerns about our wayward behaviour, and he made these concerns known to Isaiah, Jeremiah, and other prophets.

In the baptism of Jesus, we are reminded of the one who was the last in the line of prophets. We acknowledge this when we sing, "On Jordan's Bank the Baptist's Cry"; John, like the prophets of old, pointed to the coming of Jesus. At the baptism of Our Lord, the old order came to an end, and the new one began. It was the start of the ministry of Jesus, done with the full approval of God himself: "This is my Son, the beloved, with whom I am well pleased." The church was launched by God himself as Jesus came out of the waters of Jordan.

It is sad that travellers and pilgrims today cannot visit this site because of the way the Holy Land has been divided in recent years.

This lack of love and charity is far too widespread today, with certain religious groups prepared to kill those who do not conform to their beliefs and practices. Nevertheless, this is not a new thing. It has been with us for a very long time.

This is a far cry from the basic teaching of Christ, which is to love God and one another as we would wish to be loved. Is it any wonder that the church, his body, would have us ask this in the collect: "grant us, who are born again by water and the Spirit, that we may be faithful to our calling as your adopted children"?

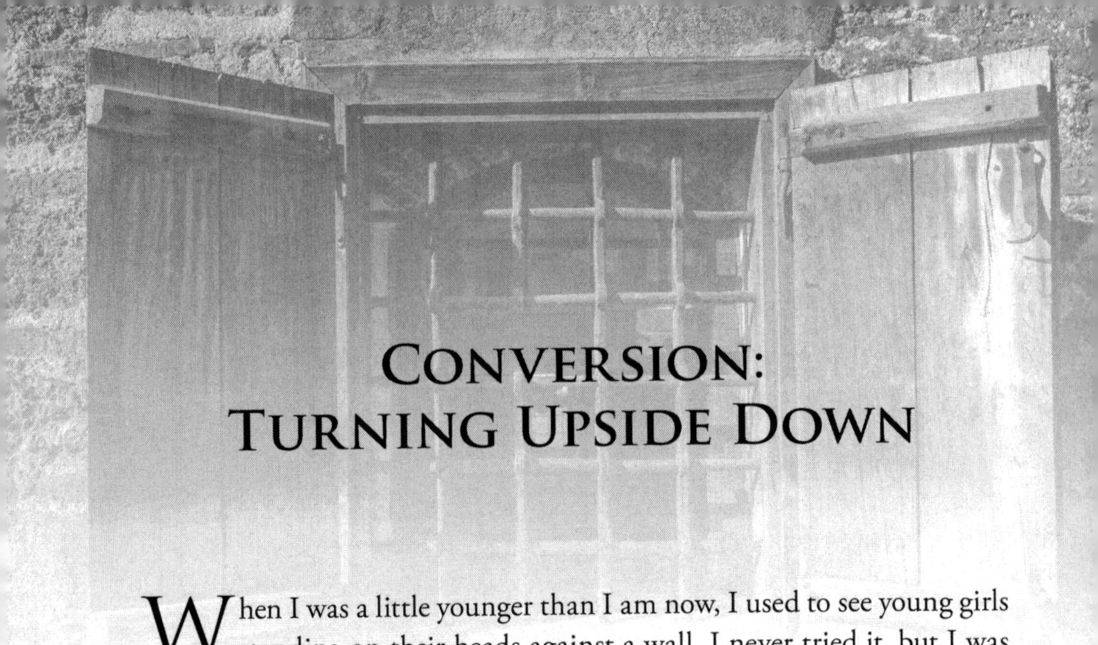

Conversion: Turning Upside Down

When I was a little younger than I am now, I used to see young girls standing on their heads against a wall. I never tried it, but I was assured that the world looked different from that position.

I was reminded of this as I thought about St Paul's conversion on the road to Damascus, which we commemorate on 25 January. In his conversion, Paul's world was turned upside down.

He was born and brought up to be a Pharisee. They were a powerful yet unofficial Jewish pressure group largely led by priests. Their aim was to purify Israel through strict observance of Jewish law (or Torah). To them, the study and practice of the law was equivalent to worshipping in the Temple. It was a strict legalistic system, which seems to some to be a long way from the teachings of Jesus, summarised as love God and love your neighbour.

We can appreciate the way Saul, prior to his conversion, saw the Christian movement as a serious threat to Judaism and his position as a Pharisee.

In his work of trying to eliminate the followers of Jesus, he must have noticed their behaviour and their words as they faced up to whatever horrors were in store. We know he was there at the stoning of St Stephen, and he must have noticed Stephen's wonderful witness to faith in Christ Jesus.

Was Paul (Saul) turning these things over in his mind as he travelled to Damascus? We will never know. However, there is no doubt that everything became clear to him in a blinding flash. His viewpoint became similar to that of those little girls years ago who viewed the world whilst standing on their heads. Jesus turned Saul's values upside down. This is what conversion is all about. Would that this could happen to all baptised Christians. The world would be transformed.

EPIPHANY

If you have studied the Greek language, you know already that the word *epiphany* essentially means "manifestation".

The Epiphany is a festival which originated in the Eastern Church in the third century. Epiphany was celebrated in honour of Our Lord's baptism, which we celebrate on the Sunday following. The Western Church, of which we are members, did not introduce it until the fourth century, and it was, as it still is today, associated with the showing of the Saviour of the world to non-Jewish people (the Gentiles), making Jesus obvious and clearly seen to us. This is a task which continues to the present day.

Then, there are those gifts: gold for a king, frankincense for a priest, and myrrh for a sacrificial victim, thereby showing us the mission and destiny of the tiny baby in that manger, that feeding trough, in Bethlehem.

Ephrem of Syria, writing in the fourth century, has this to say of the baby:

> Reconciling peace, sent to the people, gladdening Flash, who came to the gloomy, Powerful leaven (yeast) conquering all silence, Patient One, who has captured creation little by little. Blessed is he who became small without limit.

Elsewhere, Ephrem writes, "Blessed is your birth that stirred up the universe."

Yes, Jesus does have a big spoon, and he is stirring the universe now. He could do with our help.

THE PRESENTATION OF CHRIST IN THE TEMPLE (CANDLEMAS)

For many years in my church, the candles used at services and on the altars on Candlemas have first been blessed at the Eucharist. It is also the custom for members of the congregation to be given a candle at the main act of worship. All this is because when Mary and Joseph took the baby Jesus to church for Mary's purification, on what might have been his first visit to the Temple, that old gentleman, Simeon, described the baby in Mary's arms as being "a light to lighten the Gentiles". Clearly, this tiny Jewish baby was going to have a lasting influence on humanity!

It would seem that humanity needed that influence then. Herod the king, "in his raging", as the carol tells us, had hoped to learn where the baby was, in order to kill him. But those wise men were warned in a dream that Herod was up to no good and were advised to go home another way. Because he had not heard from those three wise men, this unstable king, always fearful for his own safety, had all the young children of a certain age killed.

Indeed, so frightened was Herod for his own skin that he had a palace built at Masada, on a large rocky outcrop, to which he could go if things got too hot.

One is tempted to ask if anything has changed. Looking around us in the place where we live, watching television and reading the newspapers will show that we are living in a world where selfishness and greed, bigotry and cruelty are still around. In short, people are self-centred. Maybe we should try to set an example by living as we ask in the collect:

> Grant that we may be presented to you with pure and clean hearts by your Son.

We could not have a better example to follow than that of the Son of God himself.

Lent

The word comes from an Old English word, *lencten,* which means "spring": a period of new growth and emerging life in the natural world. Our church season of Lent is one of penitence and preparation for the greatest of all Christian festivals: Easter, when we celebrate the sacrifice of Jesus on the cross for us. But, of course, Easter is all about his glorious Resurrection. Events which bring new life to us as individuals and as members of his holy church. A good time to slow down and look at our lives, our relationship with God and those with whom we live and move and have our being.

In the old days, Lent was a long, rigid fast. Only one meal each day; fish and meat were forbidden. Gradually, the extreme fast was relaxed (although, in the Orthodox [Eastern] Church, fasting remains rigorous).

Lent was also a period of preparation for baptism, when people became members of the holy church and committed to the Christian way. Today, many baptisms take place on Holy Saturday. The archbishop of York uses an inflatable bathtub to baptise people by total immersion outside York Minster. Then again, baptism plays an important part in the Easter ceremonies, which not only include baptism but also the renewal of baptismal vows. When this happens in the Minster, the font used is on the site of the baptism of Edwin, king of Northumbria, and his cousin Hild, better known to us as Hilda.

But we need a balance in all things. St Bernard of Clairvaux has this to say:

> Sorrow for sin is indeed necessary, but it should not involve endless self-preoccupation. You should dwell also on the glad remembrance of the loving kindness of God.

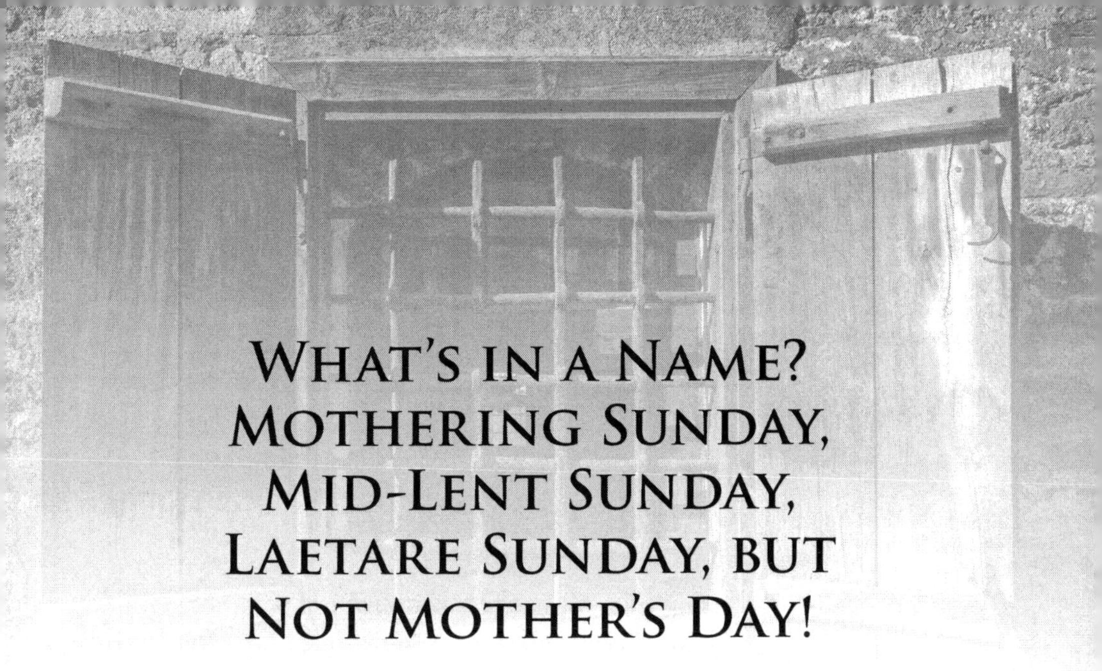

What's in a Name? Mothering Sunday, Mid-Lent Sunday, Laetare Sunday, but Not Mother's Day!

Laetare Sunday comes from the Latin words of the opening words of the Introit appointed for the day from Isaiah 44: "Rejoice ye, with Jerusalem and be glad with her, all ye that love her." Mothering Sunday because, in pre-Reformation days, it was the custom to visit Mother Church on this day. (Mother Church referred to the cathedral church of the diocese.)

It was also the day when the Pope blessed a golden rose which was then presented to monarchs and others who had served the church well, as the rose is the flower of Mary, the mother of Jesus. The rose presented to Empress Eugene in 1846 is now in Farnborough Abbey. The day is also known as "Rose Sunday", again, perhaps because the rose is the flower of Mary. Certainly because of this, we have the Rosary and rose gardens, and the system of meditations for which beads are used as a guide through the Rosary.

It is mid-Lent Sunday because it is halfway through the season and provides a brief respite during the rigors of the Lenten fast. Hence, these other words for to the day: Refreshment Sunday, Pudding Pie Sunday, and Simnel Sunday.

Whatever the name, it is good to pause and thank God for Mary, the Mother of Jesus, and her obedience to the call of God.

Today is also an opportunity to say thank you to God for Mother Church and the blessings we gain from being active members. It is also a time for us to thank God for our own mums, what they are to us and, maybe, what they have been to and for us.

But, remembering that it is Laetare Sunday, "Rejoice ye Jerusalem", we say thank you for Jerusalem, and for Jesus who bore our punishment on that "green hill without a city wall".

Join Aelred of Reivaulx in praying to Our Lord:

> I ask you, by the power of your most sweet name, and by the mystery of your holy humanity to put away my sins and heal the langours of my soul, mindful only of your goodness, not my ingratitude.

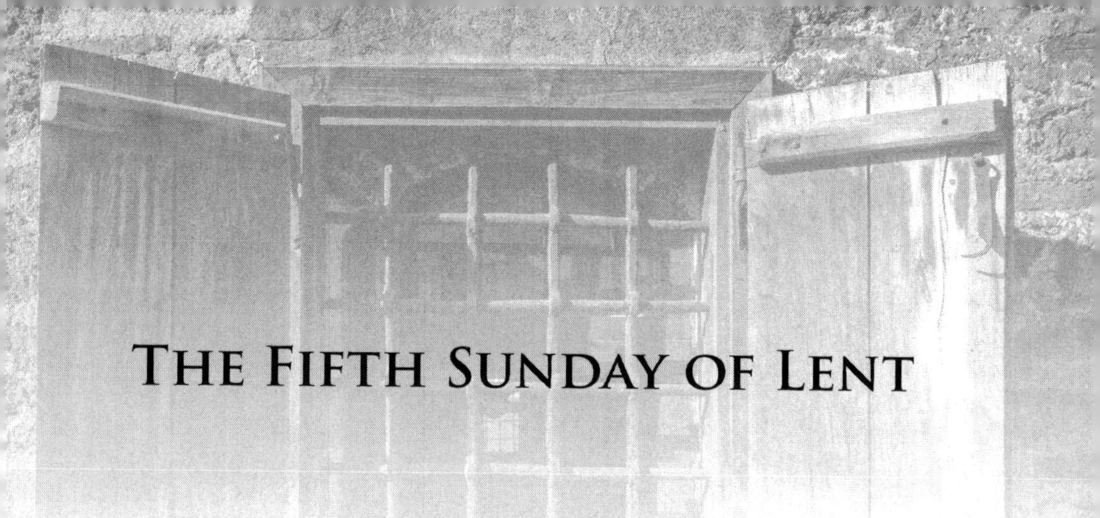

THE FIFTH SUNDAY OF LENT

Many Anglicans have become accustomed to calling the fifth Sunday of Lent Passion Sunday. A flick through the Common Worship book shows that the title "Passion Sunday" does not appear. This is partly because the Roman Catholic liturgical reforms, which followed the second Vatican Council, eliminated "Passiontide", as such, from the Kalendar, to avoid any suggestion that Passiontide is a separate season. On the contrary, it is an integral part of the Lent season (from Ash Wednesday until Easter Eve). So, in the Roman calendar, there are the first five Sundays in Lent, and the sixth one is designated "Palm Sunday of the Passion of Christ". The Anglican Common Worship book also designates the five Sundays as "Sundays in Lent", but makes life difficult be retaining the word *Passiontide* for the period from the fifth Sunday in Lent to Easter Eve.

We are getting nearer to each other—slowly. All this is to say that we enter the most solemn part of Lent as we enter into the sufferings of Our Lord as the cross gets ever closer.

(Material in this section is from "Using Common Worship—Times and Seasons".)

PASSION

Did you know that the passion flower was supposed to suggest the instruments of the passion? Then, there is passion fruit. All these relate to a remembrance of what we think and pray about during the latter part of the Lenten season.

The dictionary defines *passion* as "a strong barely controllable emotion, an outburst of anger". Maybe the naming of Passion Sunday is a reminder of God's anger concerning the ways in which humankind has behaved and of which he does not approve. The dictionary also says of passion, "the suffering of Christ during his last days". Might this be seen as the barely controllable emotion of Almighty God being worked out in his Son? For we read, "He gave his only Son so that everyone who believes in him may not be lost but have eternal life." In short, he bore our sins on his shoulders and took our punishment for us—such is the love of God for us humans. So, whatever we do that is extra in our devotions in the days leading to Easter are to help us enter into the Lord's suffering, done simply through reading scripture, making extra time for prayer, or coming to the services which lead us to the Easter season.

Whatever we may do, the words of St Ignatius Loyola meditating in front of his crucifix come to mind:

> Teach us, good Lord to serve you as you deserve; to give and not to count the cost; to fight and not to heed the wounds; to toil and not to seek for rest; to labour and not to seek for any reward, save that of knowing that we do your will.

Palm Sunday

It is quite a surprise to arrive at the top of the Mount of Olives. When Jesus was there on the first Palm Sunday, he would have looked over the valley of the Kidron Brook towards the Temple Mount. He would have seen the Temple itself and, no doubt, wept at the thought that in AD 70 it would be destroyed. If we visit, we would have a similar view. We would see the Temple Mount and an ancient wall built of huge stones. That wall is all that remains of the Temple, so, of course, we would not see the entire Temple shining in the sun. Instead, we would see two mosques: the Al-Aqsa and the Dome of the Rock. The Dome of the Rock is built over a huge stone outcrop known as Mount Moriah. It is where a well-known character from the Old Testament was commanded by God to sacrifice his son: Abraham was his name. Is there a parallel here?

As he made his way down the mountain, Jesus would have come to the Garden of Gethsemane. *Gethsemane* means "olive press". The garden is still there today, though somewhat smaller than it was in Jesus's day. There are still some very ancient-looking olive trees. The visitor is assured that they were not there on that first Holy Week, ancient though they are. Jesus also would have passed a large outcrop of rock, the site where we learn that he wept.

Dominus flavit: Jesus wept. This is commemorated in the church nearby. It has a beautiful window which looks out upon the city. The lead is fashioned to resemble a chalice and host, a reminder of the last supper he ate with his friends before his passion. The time when he said to his church as he broke the bread and poured the wine, "This is my body, this is my blood", and commanded us to "Do this to remember me."

But, on that first Palm Sunday—which we could justifiably call "Brushwood Sunday" (read the *New English Bible* translation of the Gospel of Mark to find out why)—having received welcome from the people, there was much to be done to try to increase the depth and spirituality of the then Jewish church. So, it was into the Temple to cause mayhem by scattering the tables of the money changers. It also marks Our Lord's increasing isolation as his radical ideas would become more evident.

Do you see him as a radical, a man with challenging, earth-shattering ideas and ideals? Or, are you still with "Gentle Jesus, meek and mild"? He may be a mixture of both.

Crucifixion

I was sad and sickened when I read of a boy suffering a "mock crucifixion" by his "friends" because of his Christian faith. It is so easy to let those words in the Apostles' Creed—"he was crucified, dead and buried"—roll off the tongue without a thought of the extreme cruelty of "the real thing". By which I mean not only the extreme physical pain, so graphically shown in the York Mystery Plays performed in York Minster during the summer of 2016, but also the mental anguish in the mind of the victim whilst enduring this barbarous act.

But God did this for you and me out of his love for us. All because of our sinful lack of love for him and our fellow humans. This brings to mind, yet again, that whilst meditating in front of his crucifix St Ignatius Loyola was moved to pray:

> Teach us good Lord, to serve thee as thou deservest: to give and not to count the cost; to fight and not to heed the wounds; to toil and not to seek for rest; to labour and not to ask for any reward, save that of knowing we do thy will.

But what does it mean to serve God as he deserves? Few of us would pretend that we serve him in any such way. Our service falls short of what God deserves or desires. It is more likely to be in accordance with what we find convenient. So, we, too, need to pray with St Ignatius, asking how we can serve God as he deserves. Quite a tall order for us fallen humans!

EASTER DAY

One of the readings for Easter Day tells of two people who make their way from Jerusalem to Emmaus, some three miles or so away. On their way, deep in conversation about the happenings in Jerusalem at the weekend, a person catches up with them. No doubt with his tongue in his cheek, the person asks what had happened. When they tell him, this person explains how the prophets had foretold these events. When they reached the village, good, kindly Christian folk that they were, they asked him to join them for a meal. As we know, when they reclined on their divans round the table, their guest took the bread and broke it! All at once, their eyes were opened, and they realised that it was the risen Lord. And, upon this realisation, the Man disappeared.

It is interesting that within a few hours of the Resurrection, people started going out from the city, talking among themselves and to others about the redemption of the world by Jesus. In doing so, they began to spread the Word. Also at that early stage—and indeed still today—he was known to them, as he is to us, in the breaking of bread. We are the successors of those two who made their way to Emmaus. Like those early Christians, we gain courage and strength through the reception of the Holy Sacrament of his body and blood. As the author of the epistle to the Hebrews wrote:

> Therefore since we are surrounded by so great a cloud of witnesses, let us lay aside every weight and the sin that clings so closely, looking to Jesus the pioneer and perfecter of our faith, who for the sake of the joy that was set before him endured the cross.

Jesus came to make a difference—God's difference of love—and he leaves us to continue the revolution he started.

MORE ABOUT EASTER

The date of Easter is defined as the first Sunday after the first full moon after 21 March. This was adopted by the English church at the Synod of Whitby in 662. Previously, Easter had been a fixed date in the calendar of the Celtic Church. But, at Whitby, it was decided that the church should follow the Roman way in this (and in other ways as well). It is interesting that there have been thoughts, which came from Rome, about having a fixed date for Easter. That would put the clock back!

Easter has been described as the "Queen of Festivals". It is much more important than Christmas. Maybe because it celebrates the great victory of God in overcoming death through the Resurrection of Our Lord. A death to pay for our wrongdoing and self-centredness, which deserved cruel punishment.

We say, with Gregory of Nazianzus, who lived from 329 until 389:

> Yesterday I was crucified with Christ; today I am glorified with him. Yesterday I was dead with Christ; today I am sharing in his resurrection. Yesterday I was buried with him; today I am waking with him from the sleep of death.

LOW SUNDAY

Our worship and thanksgiving reached its highpoint on Easter Sunday. Churches were lighted with many candles. There was singing and music, and, maybe, incense as well. All because, as we sing in the hymn "Jesus Christ Is Risen Today", although the shops make much of Christmas, the church knows better. Easter is the Queen of Festivals.

His earthly ministry complete, Our Lord has overcome sin and death. He has achieved his objective: sacrifice for our sins and, showing us by example and teaching, the way we, his followers, are to go.

But he left us, the church, to carry on the work he started. After all, we of the church are his body here on earth. The collect used for the Sunday after Easter in the English Book of Common Prayer leads us to pray:

> Grant us so to put away the leaven of malice and wickedness, that we may serve you in pureness of living.

Leaven is, of course the old word for yeast. It is pleasant to bake your own bread. The kitchen smells of yeast. In the process, the dough is left to rise. This is when the yeast makes a difference. It is in every part of the dough, giving it a light, fluffy feel as it gives off carbon dioxide gas.

In our lives together, Jesus would have us be like yeast in the dough, making a difference in our tiny part of God's world.

Ascension Day

Ascension Day is one of the important festivals of the church, and yet, sadly, it is mostly ignored or forgotten. In the Gospel of Luke and in the Acts of the Apostles, St Luke describes Jesus as "going up" from earth to heaven. For Jesus to ascend does not mean that he is a long way away, but, rather, that he can be—and he is—intimately present with all his people at all times. Because, in the Bible, heaven is the "control room" of earth, and this means that Jesus is actually in charge of what goes on in the here and now. His way is not the same as the ways of earthly rulers. Jesus works through faithful obedience, including the patient endurance of suffering. The life and witness of the early church resulted in the spreading of the gospel around the world, and this shows the effect of the Ascension of Our Lord. He was with them, just as he is with us now. Through their witness, aided by the risen Lord and his Holy Spirit, the faith spread throughout the world, making it truly catholic, truly universal.

Yes, he is still with us, just as he was with them. What are we waiting for?

More about Ascension Day

Going *up*.

It is easy to be confused by the words we use to explain what we are about to do or may have done. Although we go *down* south if we want to, say, visit the South Coast, if we go to London, we go *up* to the capital. Similarly, if we study for a degree, we go *up* to the university at the beginning of term and *down* at the end.

Jesus himself came *down* to earth when he was conceived of the Virgin Mary, leaving heaven to live the life of a human being and thereby showing the way that God would have us live. Also, because our heavenly Father loves us so much, Jesus came to life as a human to suffer the pain of separation from God as he hung upon the cross.

So, might it be possible that, rather than actually going up into the sky at the Ascension, he was simply returning to the existence he enjoyed, in the same way that we do when we come *down* from London to home or return home at the end of a university term?

But where does that leave you and me?

St Augustine put it rather well when he said in a sermon:

> Today our Lord Jesus Christ ascended into heaven, let our hearts ascend with him. Listen to the words of the Apostle.
>
> "if you have risen with Christ, set your hearts on things that are above where Christ is seated at the right hand of God; seek the things that are above, not the things that are on earth."

So, it would seem that he is still close at hand to give support and inspiration when needed.

Pentecost and Whitsunday

Called Whitsunday because it became a popular time for baptisms, which would be by total immersion. When baptised in this way today, as in the very early church, candidates wear a simple white robe. Because of this, the Sunday of Pentecost became known as Whitsunday—"White Sunday" if you like.

There are those who prefer the word *Pentecost* to describe this important church festival celebrating the birth of the church. This commemorates the day when the Holy Spirit of God came among those followers of Jesus. As a result, they were transformed from a group who were afraid of the Jews into the Young Church ready to go out to bear witness of their faith in the risen Lord.

You may know that Pentecost is the Greek term for the Jewish Feast of Weeks, which falls on the fiftieth day after Passover. This was a sort of harvest festival when the wheat was harvested and samples were taken to the Temple. Because the Holy Spirit descended on the apostles on this day (see Acts 2:1), the name was applied to the Christian feast commemorating when the Holy Spirit launched the church. The beginning of gathering in souls for God.

A reading of the Acts of the Apostles gives a picture of the life of those loyal followers of Jesus. We are the "descendants" of those members of the Young Church. Are we following in their footsteps? Are we following the Master's command to love him and one another as he loves us? Are we helping the Pentecost harvesting of souls?

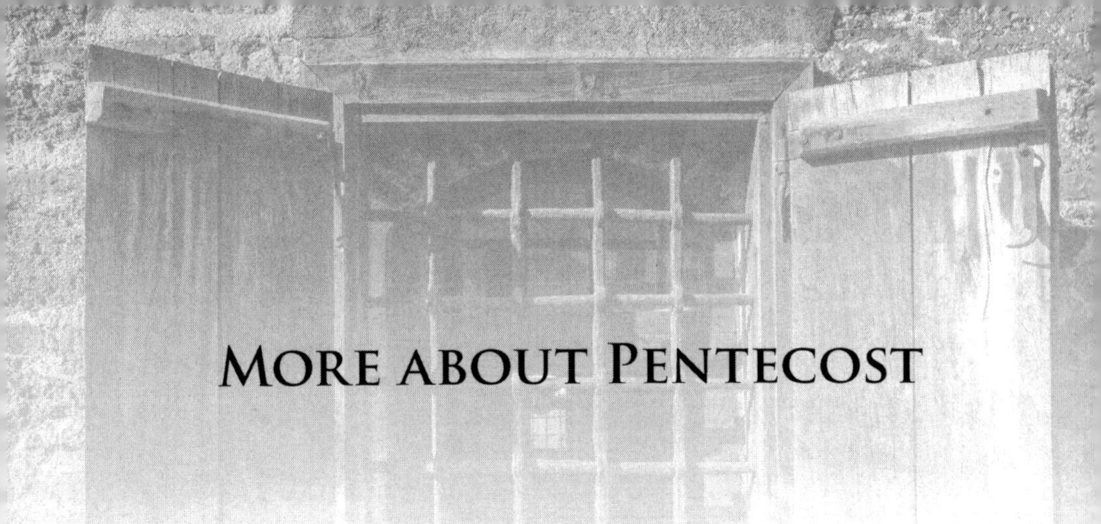

More about Pentecost

It must have been quite a day when, in that upper room, the Holy Spirit gave those followers of Jesus a shock by descending in such a way that they were shaken—nay, inspired—to be bold. Bold enough to go out into the world in which the "religious" people had generally been hostile to the teachings and actions of Jesus. But they were fired by the Spirit to adopt this attitude of mind and outlook to go out and witness to their faith in Him and convert others to his way of thinking.

Our Lord was concerned about the spiritual needs of his children. So, too, were his followers concerned with the spiritual needs of those with whom they lived and moved and had their being. Their relationships—whether they felt accepted and at peace with God, whether they suffered pain through sickness or the way others treated them. The list is a very long one. Yet, then and now, we who call ourselves Christians are called to be concerned and offer such help as we can.

Again, it is easy to go in where angels fear to tread. Possibly the most helpful thing we can do is to provide a sympathetic ear to those who need to talk, to pour out their problems and feel better for doing so. Often the hearer needs to say very little; indeed, it would be unwise to say much. We help those needing to talk by listening to them, by being an ear and remembering them in our prayers.

Here is one of the tasks to which we are called. We do not need to be ordained to do this; all we need is the strength given through our reception of his body and blood in the Holy Sacrament, through our frequent prayerful reading of the Holy Scriptures. Do not forget the Bible; it is our library and the source of our knowledge of God.

All this helps us to lead a life of faith, like those followers of Jesus who were shocked (maybe kick-started) into action at Pentecost.

Sending Out

At Pentecost, the church was essentially sent out to proclaim the gospel, and it could be said that the church sends us out at the end of every act of public worship. There are those who refer to the central act of the church, the Eucharist, as the Mass, a term used by Roman Catholic Christians and some Anglicans.

At the very end of the Roman Mass, the celebrant says, "The Mass is ended, go in peace." Apparently, this comes from a Latin word, *mittere,* which means "to send, to dismiss". So, it became applied to a service from which we are dismissed. As a result, it was o,y church and is associated with the ending of the Eucharist.

Maybe this is something we forget as we make our way home for lunch or have a cuppa before we leave church. But there is a collect which bids us to remember that God himself calls us, his church, to go out and bear witness that he was in Christ reconciling the world to himself. A very painful process involving the Crucifixion of his Son—such is the love of God for us.

So, as well as being called to witness and effectively spread the good news of the gospel, we are to be ever thankful to God for his loving act. It is in that Eucharist, or Mass, that we engage in an act of thanksgiving. I understand that the word *Eucharist* means "thanksgiving". On Sundays—indeed after every occasion when we make our Communion—we are sent out to witness in thankfulness to God for his love for us. But if we need help, we may ask for this in the lovely hymn "Guide Me, O Thou Great Redeemer".

HOLY COMMUNION

For many years on the Thursday after Trinity Sunday (the first Sunday after Pentecost), the church in her wisdom bade us to remember Holy Communion—the Eucharist, the Lord's Supper, or the Mass, depending upon which name you wish to use. Eucharist isn't a bad term to use, because it means "thanksgiving". All this in a festival called Corpus Christi, literally the body of Christ.

A feast described as commemorating the institution and gift of the Eucharist. I have come to learn that the institution of the festival was a result of the influence of St Juliana, who died in 1258. In 1264, Pope Urban IV ordered its observance, and by the fourteenth century, it had become universally observed in the Western Church. St Thomas Aquinas is said to have prepared the services.

It is to remind us of that Passover meal Our Blessed Lord Jesus ate with his close friends. There they were round the table that night, lying on couches whilst eating and enjoying their meal. Many know what happened. Maybe towards the end of the meal, Jesus took bread and in the sight of everyone broke it and commanded, "This is my body, do this in remembrance of me." Then, a little later, he poured wine into a drinking vessel of some kind in front of them all, again commanding them, "This is my blood, do this in remembrance of me." As many of us know, these are the essentials of the service. All because soon after the meal, he was subjected to a mockery of a trial and then crucified—all for you and me.

For many of us, receiving the sacrament of the Lord's body and blood is an essential part of the practice of our faith, followed closely by reading the Holy Scriptures and daily prayer. As the prayer puts it:

We thank you that in this wonderful sacrament you have given us a memorial of your passion: grant us sot to reverence the sacred mysteries of your body and blood that we may know within ourselves and show forth in our lives the fruits of your redemption.

HOLY CROSS DAY

Originally, the fish was the symbol which helped Christian folk to recognise others who were of the faith. I seem to remember being told that when the church was persecuted, people would draw the shape of a fish in the dust, in witness of their faith in Christ Jesus. In September, the holy church bids us to remember the cross upon which Jesus won our salvation. The cross is now the universal symbol of Christianity.

Constantine the Great, proclaimed Emperor of Rome in York (then called Eboracum), in 306, issued the Edict of Milan, which caused the persecution of Christian people to cease. As a result, pilgrims began to travel to Jerusalem to visit and pray at the holy sites. Those pilgrims included Helena, the mother of Constantine, who was a Christian. Whilst overseeing excavations in the city, she is said to have uncovered a cross, which many believed to be the cross of Christ. As a result, a basilica was built on the site of the Holy Sepulchre and dedicated on 14 September 335: hence, Holy Cross Day. It is still there, much enlarged, a site where Christians of all sorts go, pray, and celebrate their liturgies.

The cross is still a much-respected and revered symbol of our faith. In the collect for Holy Cross Day we pray:

> Grant us so to glory in the cross of Christ that we, may gladly suffer for his sake.

Many have suffered, and continue to suffer, for their faith in Our Blessed Lord and the cross upon which he won our salvation.

It was whilst meditating upon his crucifix that St Ignatius Loyola wrote the prayer which begins "Teach us good Lord to serve you as you deserve …".

All Saints and All Souls

When the nights draw in, November comes once again, and we put more wood on the fire or turn up the central heating. This is the time when the huge family of Christians, of which we are a part, is celebrated. In the Apostles' Creed, we state a belief in the Communion of Saints. This includes all those who have accepted Christ as their saviour and have followed him in their lives, both those living now and those now departed. You may ask what a saint looks like. There are statues and stained-glass windows in churches. If you pop into the crypt of York Minster, you will see the Roman coffin containing the remains of St William. Should you visit Durham Cathedral, you could see where St Cuthbert is buried. But to see a saint, all you have to do is look into a mirror whilst shaving or applying make-up because a saint is one of God's people. St Paul begins his letter to the church at Ephesus, "From Paul, Apostle of Christ Jesus commissioned by the will of God to the saints of God at Ephesus."

This means that all the redeemed, living and departed, are one fellowship, which death does not interrupt. So, the church keeps two days. On the first day of the month, All Saints, remembering all Christian people of whatever sort living and witnessing today; and the following day, All Souls, our brothers and sisters who have died.

When Henry VIII died, the Church of England produced its "first prayer book". It bids us to praise God for:

> [T]he wonderful grace and virtue, declared in all Thy saints from the beginning of the world: and chiefly in the glorious and most blessed Virgin Mary, mother of

> Thy Son Jesus Christ our Lord and God, and the holy patriarchs, prophets and martyrs.

There are those of us who are comforted to know that we are still one with those who have lived for and are now at rest in Christ.

But the question arises, what is being a saint all about? I came across this the other day:

> For me to be a saint means to be myself. Therefore the problem of sanctity and salvation is in fact the problem of finding out who I am and my true self.

I suspect that Jesus has a hand in this and will be able to help; it needs praying about.

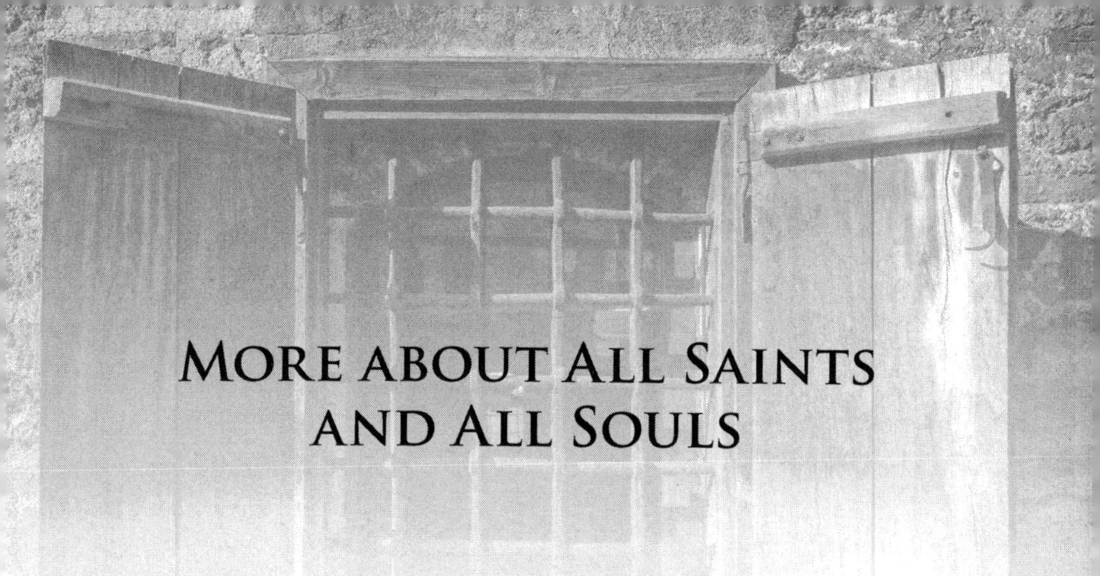

More about All Saints and All Souls

When we celebrate All Saints and All Souls, we celebrate the fulfilment of Pentecost in those men and women, known and unknown, who, wherever and whenever they lived, are now "with God". In honouring them, we acknowledge that salvation is open to all: the idea that St John strove to express when he referred to "the great multitude which no man could number, from every nation, from all tribes and people and tongues, standing before the throne and before the Lamb." This is what we celebrate at this time.

We do not know the origins of this festival. The first mention of the day being on 1 November comes from England, where the feast was introduced in the first quarter of the eighth century, probably by St Egbert of York. What is certain is that Alcuin of York, then abbot of Tours, wrote to his friend Arn, bishop of Saltsburg, about the solemnity of All Saints, which he was in the habit of celebrating on 1 November.

In doing this, we remember that huge number of folks who followed Christ in their lives and those of us who follow him today. Because we, with them, are part of the Communion of Saints in which we confess our belief every time we say the Apostles' Creed.

All Souls, on the other hand, seems to have started in Spain in 636. There is a record of a Requiem celebrated as early as 1075 in England. Prayers for the dead are recommended by the Book of Maccabees. From early Christian times, there is evidence of the practice of remembering the departed in prayer—on inscriptions in the catacombs in Rome, for example.

So, on this day, we join the rest of Christendom in thanking God for the whole of his family and praying that the souls of the departed may rest in peace and rise in glory.

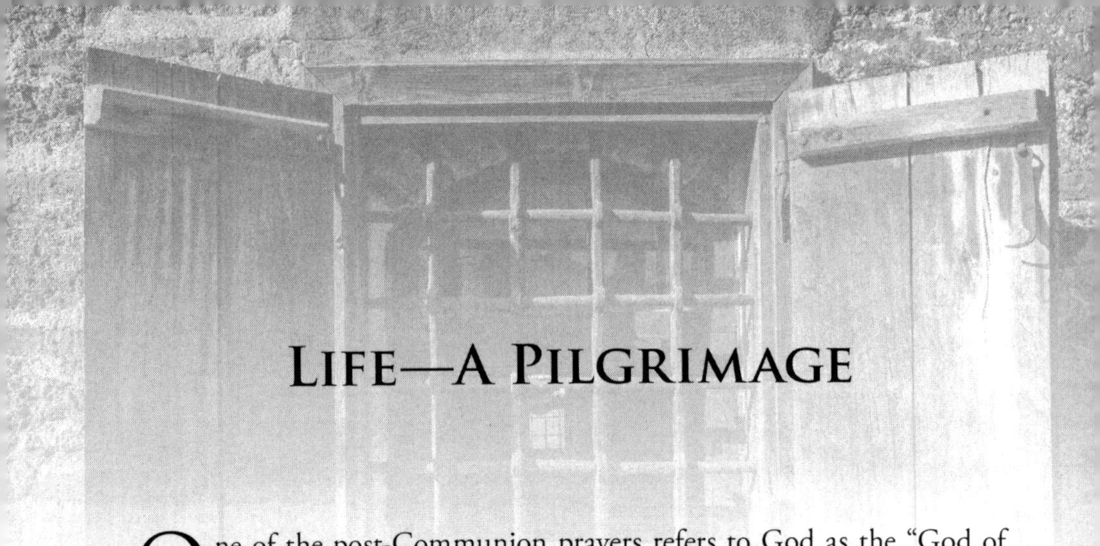

LIFE—A PILGRIMAGE

One of the post-Communion prayers refers to God as the "God of our pilgrimage", painting a picture in our minds of a life lived close to him, of a journey leading to a full life in him, which may begin whilst we are on the way..

People go on "holy journeys" today. Journeys taken out of their devotion to God. The practice of visiting places associated with the life of Christ was encouraged when the Empress Helena, mother of Constantine, visited Jerusalem in 326.

Today, people still travel to Israel to visit the holy places, the Church of the Holy Sepulchre, the Mount of Olives, and the place of transfiguration, to mention a few.

Here at home, people often go to the shrine of St Thomas of Canterbury or the shrine of Our Lady of Walsingham. There are those who still find Walsingham a place of deep spirituality.

But, as the prayer reminds us, we are on the pilgrimage of life. One in which Bible, prayer, and sacrament are our guides and food for the journey. Inevitably, we come across fellow pilgrims on the way who may need a hand to help them face the rest of the journey. This is, of course, where fellow pilgrims can help. Yet we need not fear this journey, for, as Augustine wrote:

> You are walking now by faith, still on pilgrimage in a mortal body away from the Lord; but he to whom your steps are directed is himself the sure and certain way for you.

AUTUMN: HARVEST THOUGHTS

Every year, at least in spirit, we "plough the fields and scatter the good seed on the land". This is aided by the work of many agricultural chemists, pathologists, and specialists in plant nutrition, who help the farmers and gardeners ensure that their crops are grown with the highest yields per acre. Up-to-date machinery for the cultivation of the soil and seedbed preparation, machinery for spraying the crops to eradicate pests and diseases, and other such advances help as well. All this is part of ensuring a maximum yield to feed this grossly overpopulated planet of ours, using God's gifts to the full.

Foods we buy in the supermarket, carefully packed in see-through wrappings, seem a far cry from the combine harvester, the milking parlour, and the abattoir from where some of our food comes.

Food is transported great distances. In winter, grapes may come from South Africa, whilst lettuce and other salad greens may come from Spain. It was not too long ago that such foods were seasonal; and we accepted it too.

Have we got it right? Are we here living a life of luxury at the expense of other countries where many do not know where the next meal is coming from? Think of the massive problems faced when refugees and persons fleeing from persecution need to be fed.

So, at harvest-time, let us thank God for the blessings of harvest, being mindful of our stewardship of these gifts which it brings. Let us ask him to give us his grace, his power of love, and out of that love, to help us to be careful of our use of food, avoiding any waste and, wherever possible, helping and supporting those agencies which feed the hungry and the homeless. Meanwhile, we owe Almighty God a huge thank-you for making the harvest happen and giving us his example of self-giving love.

MORE ABOUT HARVEST AND OTHER FESTIVALS

In the Book of Esther (9:22) we read, "as the days on which the Jews gained relief from their enemies, and as the month that had been turned for them from their enemies, as the month that had been turned for them from sorrow into gladness and from mourning into a holiday, that they should make them days of feasting and gladness, days for sending gifts of food to one another and gifts for the poor."

So, in our practice of keeping holidays—Easter, the greatest of all Christian festivals; Pentecost, when we remember the coming of the Holy Spirit to kick-start the church into action; and Christmas—we are following customs deeply rooted in scripture.

Every autumn, we remember with great thankfulness the safe bringing in of the harvest. We usually associate this with the grain harvest of wheat, barley, and oats. In fact, the harvest is brought in by fishermen, by those who harvest vegetables for our use through the year, by those who milk the cows—the list is a long one.

Harvest is a relatively late commemoration in the calendar of the church. It was a festival which became common as late as the mid-nineteenth century, perhaps replacing the "harvest home" celebrations which followed the bringing in of the last cartload of the harvest for stacking in the stackyard to await threshing. We thank God for the harvest, not only for our own needs but also for the hungry, the destitute, and the homeless. In the days of harvest home, harvest involved the whole community going into the fields for the back-breaking work of binding up the corn into sheaves and stacking them up north/south against each other to form stooks. When dry, they went to the stackyard. No harvest meant hungry folk. Tesco was not around the corner.

A Useful Prayer

With pilgrims in mind, this is a prayer you may know:

God be in my head, and in my understanding;
God be in my eyes, and in my looking;
God be in my mouth, and in my speaking;
God be in my heart, and in my thinking;
God be at my end, and at my departing.

This is an old prayer, a copy of which has been found in a Book of Hours dated 1514 in the library of Clare College Cambridge. It may have been used as a preparation before a service and is a real beauty.

It is the prayer of a person who humbly recognises his or her entire dependence upon God. It is a prayer that asks God to enter the daily life of that person—heart and mind, sight and speech, until the final process, that of death itself.

It is interesting that the word *depart* means to "weigh anchor" and "set sail". It is about when we put out to sea on our homeward journey to God. As Alfred, Lord Tennyson wrote, "For though from out our bourne of Time and Place the floods may bear me far, I hope to see my Pilot face to face when I have crossed the bar."

Quite a testimony of faith; a good prayer to use regularly.

Sir Jacob Astley's Prayer

> O Lord, thou knowest how busy I must be this day. If I forget thee, do thou not forget me.

Sir Jacob is said to have used this prayer on 23 October 1642. This was before Edgehill, the first battle in the civil war between the king and Parliament. Should this be true, we can sympathise with Sir Jacob. It is a prayer of a busy man and is thus a prayer for busy people. Most of us today are also busy people, or think we are. Indeed, in a world in which it is perceived that so much waits to be done, we all ought to busy. To be busy is better than being idle, for all sorts of reasons.

Yet busyness is not a virtue. It can become a fault. It is possible to be overly busy, to have too many irons in the fire. As we may be aware, it is possible to do a lot and achieve little.

Getting priorities right is part of this. Think of when Jesus went to Bethany to have a meal with Martha and Mary. Martha was so busy preparing the meal that she had little time to talk with the Lord and was cross with Mary for spending so much time talking to him.

Maybe we and the Marthas of this world need to say this prayer, which is said to have been written by a medieval monk:

> Lord temper with tranquillity our manifold activity, that we may do our work for thee with great simplicity.

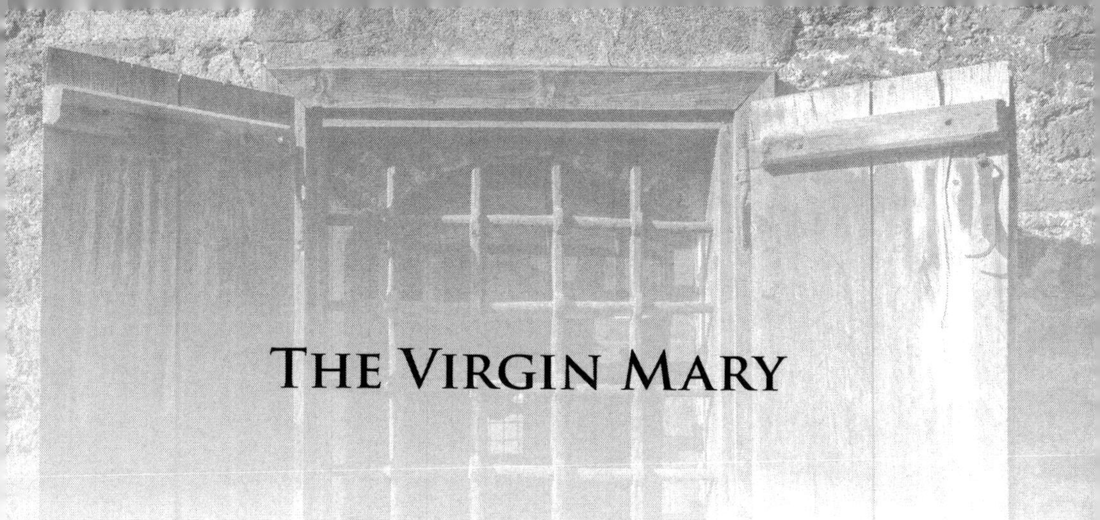

THE VIRGIN MARY

In August and on other dates in the year, the church remembers Mary, the Mother of Our Lord. The Church of England celebrate her day just as "The Virgin Mary". Our fellow Orthodox Christians call her day her "Dormition"—that is, Mary's falling asleep or death. Our brothers and sisters in Christ of the Roman Catholic Church call it her "Assumption", because they believe that on her death, Our Lady Mary was taken to heaven. There is little information in the scriptures to help us in the matter. But, one thing is certain; she was, by her obedience to the call of God, "the handmaid of the Lord". She, by that obedience, enabled the incarnation to happen: God becoming man in Jesus. For this alone, she deserves our respect. Every time we say, "Hail Mary full of grace, the Lord is with thee", we are remembering the words of the angel who announced that God would become man on that first Christmas. He also warned her what was to come. We go on in the prayer to ask, "Holy Mary Mother of God, pray for us sinners now and in the hour of our death."

She is special, but her prayers have the same power as yours or mine: she, like us, is part of the Communion of Saints, and all her prayers, like ours, approach the throne of God through Jesus, our mediator and guide. Nevertheless, we thank God for Our Lady Mary as we say a Hail Mary in her honour.

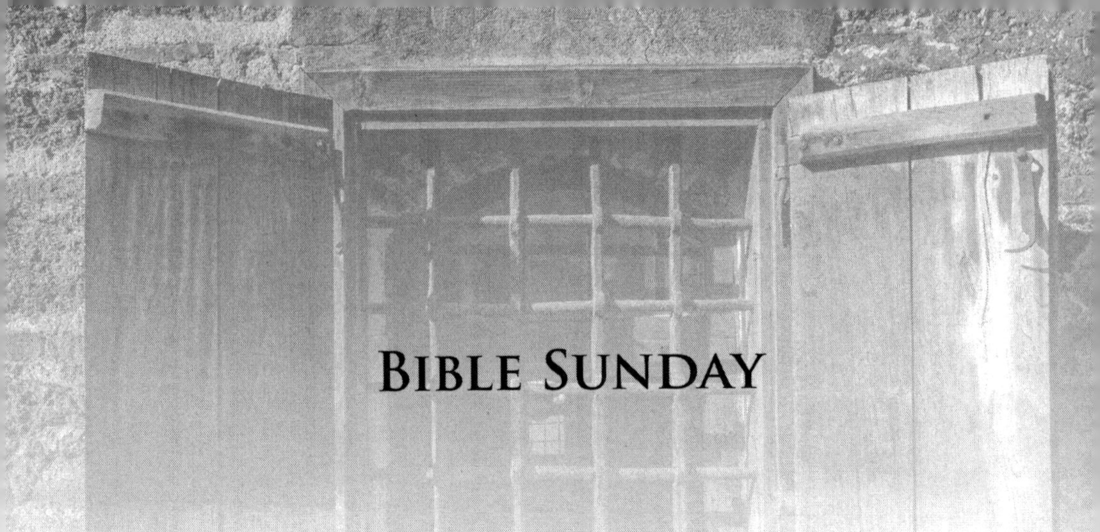

BIBLE SUNDAY

There were Anglo-Saxon gospels, also psalms and translations of parts of the Bible, though they were sometimes shortened. From about 1250, Middle English metrical translations of certain books of the Bible, especially the Psalms, were in existence. In the fourteenth century, several anonymous translations, apparently under the influence of John Wycliffe, appeared. They exist in two versions: one published in 1390, and another published later. The Council of Oxford in 1407 prohibited the making of any fresh translations of the whole or parts of the Bible.

Then came the Reformation. The first translations made directly from the original languages were the word of William Tyndale. His New Testament was printed on the Continent in 1526. The translation with which so many of us are familiar is the so-called *Authorised Version,* which was published in 1611.

Since then, a number of translations have appeared, including the *New English Bible.* So, today, we are richly blessed in having this library of books easily available on our bookshelves. Do we let them gather dust?

As those who are familiar with the contents of their pages will be aware, these books serve as an inspiration to strive for better things as well as an opportunity to learn what God's will for us is—and not just for us but for all our fellow Christians who are members of other churches. We do well to remember this as we try to carry out his command to love him and our fellow humans as we would love ourselves.

GRACE

There is at least one prayer in which we ask God to help us to perceive and know what things we ought to do and be given the grace and power to fulfil them.

It is one thing to ask for God's grace; but what, in plain words, are we asking for? I came across these descriptions of what grace is:

> [T]he love and mercy given to us by God because God desires us to have it, not because of anything we have done to earn it.
>
> [T]he benevolence shown by God to the human race.

We receive grace when we pray, when we delve into the Bible, and when God calls us to church to receive his body and blood in the Holy Sacrament.

It is significant that, to the people of Jesus's day, blood meant life. This is understandable; after all, the living cells of our bodies would not last long without a continual supply of food and oxygen, all, of course, supplied by the blood.

So, in receiving the sacrament, we are receiving the life-giving presence of God, because of his love for the human race. We are receiving the grace to help us live as he would have us live. This involves loving God and our neighbours. Which is a way of summarising all those things we do day in day out to help our fellow humans and all the animal and plant species who share this planet with us. Even if this is often very inconvenient!

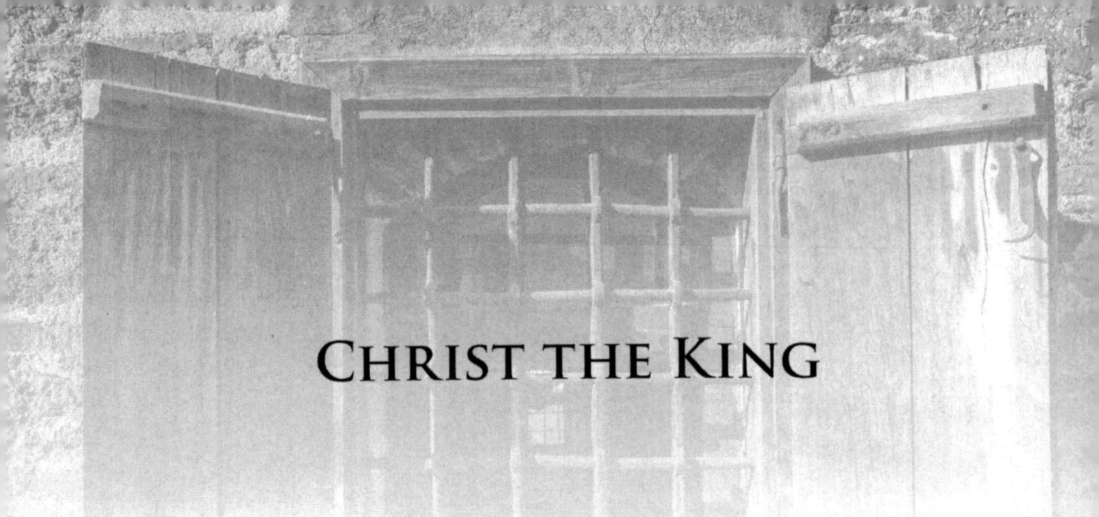

CHRIST THE KING

There are those of us who believe that we celebrate the kingship of Christ when we remember his Ascension. His return to Father's right hand after he had died for us on the cross at Calvary, thereby suffering the punishment that was ours: utter separation from God. That is why he shouted those words from the cross: "My God, My God, why have you forsaken me?"

But now we celebrate the Feast of Christ the King! This is a new festival instituted by the Roman Catholic Church in 1925 to celebrate the "all-embracing authority of Christ", as *The Oxford Dictionary of the Christian Church* puts it.

Since 1970, this festival has been kept on the last Sunday before the beginning of Advent. Anglicans have "borrowed" (or even stolen this!) from their friends in Rome.

So, it is on this day that we thank God for Jesus. It is also good to feel that when this day is kept, a huge number of Christian people are united in honouring our Saviour as King.

As the prayer appointed for use at Roman Catholic Morning Prayer leads us to pray:

> Almighty and ever living God, it is your will to unite the entire universe under your beloved Son, Jesus Christ, the King of Heaven and earth. Grant freedom to the whole creation, and let it serve your majesty forever.

Doubting Thomas

Thomas had to wait for God's timing. When Jesus went to Bethany after the death of Lazarus, Thomas said that he was wrong. Lazarus was dead, Thomas affirmed; most significantly, Thomas was slow to believe that Jesus had actually risen from the dead. But, one week later, Thomas's thoughts are overcome by Our Lord giving him the proof he needed.

We may have to wait longer than a week for God to make real what he has promised. Abraham had to wait twenty-five years for Isaac. His mother, Monica, prayed for twenty-two years for the conversion of her son, Augustine of Hippo (later St Augustine).

We can be sure that God will honour his promises. As St Augustine wrote:

> God established a time for his promises and a time for their fulfilment.

The time for promises was in the time of the prophets, until John the Baptist; from John until the end is the time of fulfilment.

More about Thomas and Doubting

It has always seemed to me unfair and unwise to look down on Thomas because he doubted the news of Jesus's Resurrection. I am sure that if I had been there, I, too, would have wanted positive proof that it had really happened. I would have, in those circumstances, found it hard to spread the gospel without having concrete proof as to what had happened.

Surely, it is a good thing that we question and challenge the many ideas—religious, political, and social—with which we are bombarded each day. In the matter of faith, it is essential that we are sure of what we believe and are able to give reasons for the faith we profess.

You may wonder why I take this point of view. The reason is (I believe) I was trained in science, where everything needs to be challenged; otherwise, things could go wrong.

A faith of which we are sure is one upon which we can base our lives and make a success of them and, hence, of that faith we profess.

St Gregory the Great wrote this:

> After his resurrection Jesus allowed this disciple to doubt, and did not desert him in his doubt. He became a witness to the reality of the resurrection. Let us rejoice at what follows "Blessed are they who have not seen and have believed the message is for us, but only if we follow up our faith with good works."

So, don't be afraid to question; sometimes it is the only way to understanding.

PREJUDICE

Once, Jesus was invited to dinner by a Pharisee. In New Testament times, dining out involved the washing of feet and reclining on couches around the table to eat the meal. It is amusing to look at Leonardo da Vinci's painting, *The Last Supper,* which is in the Cathedral of Milan. Here they all are, sitting round a table, just as would today. The artist has great difficulty in showing St John leaning on Jesus's chest. But I digress! Here they were at the Pharisee's house, reclining at table, when along came a lady of "questionable" character who proceeded to wash the Lord's feet and anoint them with expensive perfume. As we read, the Pharisee made sarcastic comments about the woman and what she was doing.

Jesus, in his wise and winning way, tells a story and leaves the Pharisee to judge, and in doing so, see where he is wrong. Many of us show prejudice. If he were here in the flesh, Our Lord would have similar words to say to you and me. But isn't it all to do with loving God and your neighbour as you would like to be loved?

Bernard of Clairvaux put it well when he wrote:

> This divine love is sincere, for it is the love of one who does not seek his own advantage. To whom is such love shown?

It is written, "When we were still his enemies, we were reconciled to God. God has loved us and has loved us freely, while we were enemies."

We have this great example in Jesus, who spoke of himself and his sacrifice when he said, "Greater love has no one than this, that a man lay down his life for his friends."

Maybe we can claim friendship with him. Thanks be to God!

ARMISTICE

As the days become shorter and the weather becomes colder, we remember the two world wars in which our country and empire were engaged, first from 1914 to 1918 and again from 1939 to 1945.

It must have been a very great relief for all when, at the eleventh hour on the eleventh day of the eleventh month in 1918, an armistice was signed to end that dreadful slaughter of people on all sides. What advantage is there for those engaged in warfare? Not being a politician or leader of the armed forces of the crown, I am not qualified to answer. It has frequently been my task to read the names of those fell, those from our parish who were killed. Each time, I want to cry. Each one a member of a family, loved by relatives at home and missed as a result of war.

I wonder how Our Lady Mary felt as she stood at the foot of the cross on that first Good Friday whilst her son hung there, dying. All because of us humans who found it difficult to love God and our neighbours as we would wish to be loved.

We wring our hands in sorrow and grief when we hear of such things, and then we try to build a better world. There is little wonder that the church directs us to pray using a prayer updated from the Book of Common Prayer:

> Heavenly Father, whose blessed Son was revealed to destroy the works of the devil and to make us the children of God and heirs of eternal life, grant that we, having this hope, may purify ourselves even as he is pure that when he shall appear in power and great glory we may be made like him.

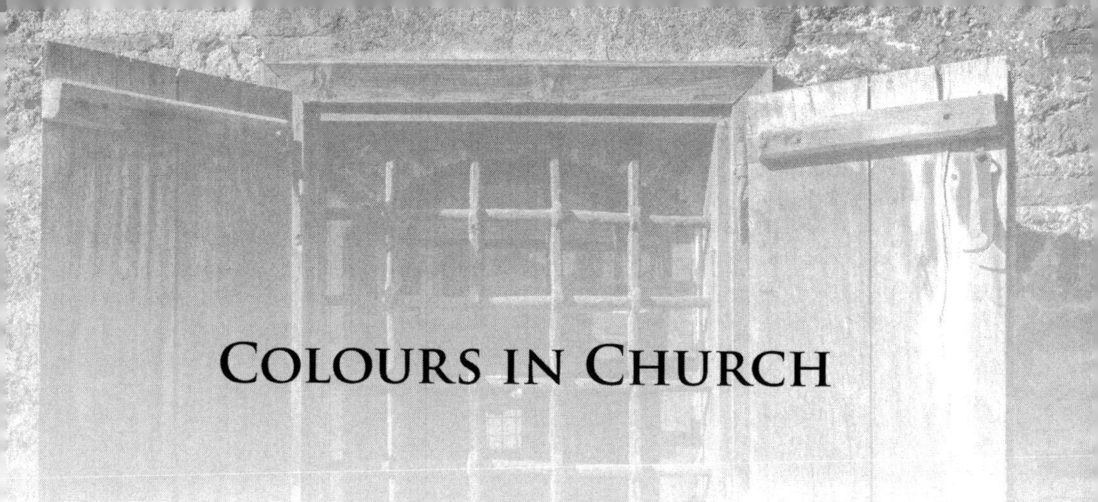

COLOURS IN CHURCH

Everything that is done in church has meaning and is there with the intention of helping us, the worshippers, focus on to the particular theme, event, or teaching at the centre of the service each Sunday. Hence, during Advent and Lent, the colour of the altar frontal, and the stole and chasuble worn by the priest celebrating the Eucharist, is violet or purple, because this is a season of reflection and penance. Just to be confusing, some churches, of which York Minster is one, use blue for these seasons.

Easter is white, or, if the church has some, cloth of gold, symbolising the joy and magnificence of Easter—which is, after all, the Queen of Festivals. Similarly, red is the colour for martyrs, those who shed their blood in defence of the faith of Christ. Red is also used for the feast of Pentecost, or Whitsun, reminding us of the coming of the Holy Spirit in tongues of living flame on that first Pentecost Day, inflaming those followers of Christ with zeal to go out and witness for the faith that was in them.

Green is used for the long Trinity season. Black is for requiems for the departed.

The first recorded use of liturgical colours is that of Augustinian canons in Jerusalem. The use of colours can be a useful aid for worshippers. The danger is to concentrate too much on the correctness of the colour used, causing worshippers to be distracted from what really matters: a worthy offering of an act of worship. Hence, the practice in some churches is not to use liturgical colours. If used rightly, they can help us to offer a worthy sacrifice of praise to the throne of God.

St Luke

St Paul describes Luke as "the beloved physician". In his second letter to Timothy, Paul describes Luke as his only companion in prison.

Luke writes as a non-Jew, as a Gentile. In his gospel, he makes it clear that the good news of salvation is a worldwide—a catholic—message to all, regardless of gender, social position, or nationality. This is, of course, as relevant to us today as it was in those early days when the Apostle Paul was working hard to convert those living in the area of the eastern Mediterranean.

Paul and Luke, together, brought healing and faith to the people, whomever they were and from wherever they came. We are their successors, and we are here to spread the gospel by word and example, wherever we may find ourselves. I came across this surprising quote from Gregory the Great:

> The world is full of priests, and yet it is rare that you will find them at work in God's harvest.

These are strong words which I would not dare to quote in the presence of my ordained friends! We are all aware of the acute shortage of priests, and one wonders what laypeople can do about it. (I suppose they could offer themselves for ordination!)

Seriously, the list is a long one. But, suffice it to say, we can provide support and companionship for the lonely and help for the needy. Quite importantly, we can listen! We have time to let those who are "uptight", or burdened with sorrow and guilt, use us as shoulders to lean on and kind ears to listen when they simply talk. All we need to do is listen, provide companionship—just be there, just listen without moralising to anyone who needs to unburden themselves of worries which threaten to overwhelm them. Should the person feel that the guilt is unbearably heavy, then a priest is called so that, after confession, he can deliver absolution with a penance.

Being Called

There is an Anglican collect which asks, "Hear our prayer for all your faithful people, that in their vacation and ministry they may serve you in holiness and truth." We usually refer to a priest being "called" to his or her ministry by God himself. It is a sobering thought that all of us who profess and call ourselves Christian are called to serve him in his church, in whatever capacity.

I ask myself, if I am aware of my calling and making a worthy response to that calling. I also ask myself, as well as you, for help in knowing what God wants me to do in response to his call.

I found these words helpful in my dilemma:

> God, we know, loves us and takes care of what he has fashioned. He is the fountain of wisdom and he knows what to do to promote our welfare, and nothing is beyond his power. Hence, we must be convinced that all he does is for our benefit and we ought to receive it with gratitude.

So, this is not a one-sided association. We can and do rely on our heavenly Father to help us in our daily witness to him—through Bible, sacrament, and prayer, so that we can serve him in holiness and truth. The church in the wide world needs our witness and devotion. It is this to which God calls us. The way in which we deliver our witness depends to the sort of ministry he calls us to: priestly, lay, or as a living part of the church in the world.

Sources

The Concise Oxford Dictionary of the Christian Church
© E. A. Livingstone, 1977, 2000, 2006, 2013
The moral rights of the authors have been asserted.

Celebrating the Saints: Daily Spiritual Readings for the Calendar of the Church of England
© Robert Atwell, 1998, 1999, 2004, 2016

Celebrating the Seasons. Daily Spiritual Readings for the Christian Year.
© Robert Atwell, 2000

St. John the Baptist. Quote from Augustine. Celebrating the Saints. Canterbury Press page 212.

Christmas Thoughts. Ephrem of Syria. Celebrating the Seasons. Canterbury Press page 43.

Christmas again John 1,1 Authorised Version of the Bible.

Eiphany. Celebrating the Seasons pages 64 and 68.

Presentation of Christ in the Temple. (Candlemas). The text should read in the reference to Masada "he had a palace built at Masada."

Lent, quote at the end. Celebrating the Seasons. page 148.

Mid Lent (Mothering) Sunday. Aelred of Reivaulx quote Celebrating the Seasons page 182.

Passion. Prayer of St. Ignatius Loyola. Prayers that live. Frank Colquhoun SPCK.

Easter Day quote from Hebrews not identified.

More about Easter. Gregory of Nazianus. Celebrating the Seasons page 222.

More about Ascension Day, going up. Augustine, Celebrating the Seasons page 275.

Harvest and other festivals. Esther 9 v, 22 The New English Bible.

A useful prayer. Prayers that live. Frank Colquhoun.

Sir Jacob Astley's Prayer. Prayers that live. Frank Colquhoun.

About Thomas doubting. Quote from St. Gregory. Celebrating the Saints page 226.

Prejudice. St. Bernard. Celebrating the Seasons page 330.

St. Luke. Celebrating the Saints page 383.

About the Author

I am a retired teacher of secondary-school children. In 1960, I was admitted to the Anglican Office of Reader. Happily, I am still active in this work in my parish church. On retirement in 1982, I became a guide at York Minster, soon afterwards becoming an honorary chaplain. As of this writing, I am still fulfilling these duties.

Printed and bound by CPI Group (UK) Ltd, Croydon, CR0 4YY